WORLDVIEW GUIDE

WUTHERING HEIGHTS

Marcus Schwager

canonpress
Moscow, Idaho

Published by Canon Press
P.O. Box 8729, Moscow, Idaho 83843
800.488.2034 | www.canonpress.com

Marcus Schwager, *Worldview Guide for Wuthering Heights*
Copyright ©2019 by Marcus Schwager.
Cited page numbers come from the Canon Classics edition of the book (forth-
coming), www.canonpress.com/books/canon-classics.

Cover design by James Engerbretson
Cover illustration by Forrest Dickison
Interior design by Valerie Anne Bost and James Engerbretson

Printed in the United States of America.

Schwager, Marcus, author.
Wuthering Heights worldview guide / Marcus Schwager.
Moscow, Idaho : Canon Press, [2019].
LCCN 2019011313 | ISBN 9781947644304 (paperback : alk. paper)
LCSH: Brontèe, Emily, 1818-1848. Wuthering Heights.
LCC PR4172.W73 S39 2019 | DDC 823/.8--dc23
LC record available at https://lccn.loc.gov/2019011313

A free end-of-book test and answer key are available for download at
www.canonpress.com/ClassicsQuizzes

19 20 21 22 23 24   9 8 7 6 5 4 3 2 1

CONTENTS

INTRODUCTION

Silent is the house: all are laid asleep:

One alone looks out o'er the snow-wreaths deep,

Watching every cloud, dreading every breeze

That whirls the wildering drift, and bends the
groaning trees.[1]

Mysterious curses pass through a secluded family in Yorkshire's chilly, windswept moors. Hidden torment and misguided passions spell eventual doom for two prominent households. The haunted, tangled tale of *Wuthering Heights* continues to captivate readers by the hundreds, thousands, and millions—a tale reflecting family misfortune its author knew all too well.

---

1. From "The Visionary" by Emily Brontë. Poetic lines opening this and coming sections are taken from the following: *The Works of Charlotte, Emily, and Anne Brontë in the Twelve Volumes: Poems of Currer, Ellis, and Acton Bell with Cottage Poems by Patrick Brontë, Vol III* (London: J. M. Dent and Co., 1893).

THE WORLD AROUND

To-day, I will seek not the shadowy region;

Its unstaining vastness waxes drear;

And visions rising, legion after legion,

Bring the unreal world too strangely near.

In 1837, at eighteen years of age, Victoria became queen of a tumultuous British realm. Early political power-jockeying and labor unrest (specifically child labor and coal mining conditions) made the public unhappy with the governing class, but a series of assassination attempts by various vigilantes rallied the people in defense of their noble lady. She married Prince Albert three years after being crowned, and the two built a large family together (nine children in all). In 1845, two years before *Wuthering Heights* was published, a potato blight devoured Ireland. Over one million Irish died in the Great Famine, and an even greater number emigrated to other countries, many to America. Although the queen donated more than any other private individual to the relief, the Irish considered it vastly insufficient, given their dire straits. Many Irish referred to her not as a noble and mythical Faerie Queen but as a distant and heartless Famine Queen. Over time, Queen Victoria's political place and popularity grew and prospered, making her one of England's most loved monarchs, but the early years of her reign (when the Brontë sisters were preparing and publishing their works) were challenging indeed.

The American and European world of the 1830s and 40s saw concurrent expansion abroad as well as factions within. For Europe, much of the expansion was overseas, with France taking Algiers and England becoming a growing presence in the Middle East, India, and China. Many European countries would experience significant revolutions by 1850. Most revolutions were repressed while some led to new states, such as Greece winning independence from the Ottoman Empire in 1830. In America, expansion went west. Besides many new states and territories explored and settled, Texas won independence from Mexico in its own revolution, becoming the Republic of Texas (soon to be annexed as a state). This led to the Mexican-American War; a U.S. victory established Texas and yielded further territories from Mexico stretching to the Pacific Ocean (where gold fever would soon overtake thousands in California). Despite a great American expansion, fomenting seeds were liberally sown throughout the country over the increasingly divisive subjects of slavery and states' rights.

ABOUT THE AUTHOR

Sometimes I seem to see thee rise;

A glorious child again;

All virtues beaming from thine eyes

That ever honored men.[2]

Emily Jane Brontë was born on July 30, 1818 to Maria Branwell and Patrick Brontë, an Irish-born man who studied theology at Cambridge and, after being ordained as a priest, spent his remaining years in England. Emily was the fourth of their six children: Maria (b. 1814), Elizabeth (b. 1815), Charlotte (b. 1816), Branwell (b. 1817), Emily (1818), and Anne (b. 1820). The children had little time to enjoy maternal affections as their mother died in 1821.

---

2. From Emily Brontë's "The Wanderer From the Fold." Though it does not state so explicitly, this may be a poetic meditation on her brother's promising youth contrasted by his destructive adult addictions.

Even on his modest income, Reverend Brontë encouraged his children's education, sending his daughters to the Cowan Bridge School for Clergymen's Daughters. Unfortunately, the school was dreadfully cold in its inhospitable austerity. The disciplines and privations were often heartless, the food was poorly prepared, and the circumstances encouraged depression and sickness. In 1825, young Maria and Elizabeth both died after contracting tuberculosis on the heels of other sicknesses (like typhoid fever) sweeping the school. Rev. Brontë decided to educate his son, Branwell, and remaining daughters, Charlotte, Emily, and Anne, at home. There the young siblings loved to weave mystical tales for one another, listen to local Yorkshire legends, and explore the moors about them. Many people find little delight in moorlands, for they are generally barren, supporting very little plant life. In fact, in England moors are often simply called "wastelands." Emily, however, rooted her very soul in the moor, and would fall anxious and ill if ever leaving it for long. She tried leaving home for another school in 1836, but left the school after six months. Then, in 1842, she tried to leave again, traveling to study in Brussels, Belgium; again, she did not last a year, the call of her homeland too heavy upon her.

The siblings' writing aspirations covered prose and verse. In 1846, they assembled their best poetry and published jointly under pseudonyms to guard their own identities (Emily took the name "Ellis Bell"). That first edition of poetry was a publishing failure as it sold only two copies and brought the sisters little attention. But the work of organizing and collecting their work may have done them some good as they each had a novel to offer for publication within a year (Charlotte finally finding publishers after countless refusals). Emily Brontë's *Wuthering Heights* published in December of 1847, at the same time Anne's *Agnes Grey* released, and just two months after Charlotte's *Jane Eyre*. Unlike the poetry, their prose works sold well and launched their literary careers.

But another force was working unseen in the background. Branwell, who showed some early promise as an artist and writer, flirted and finally wedded addiction. He grew increasingly weak and wild. *Webster's Biographical Dictionary* puts it succinctly: "Patrick Branwell, drunkard and opium addict, was a burden and humiliation to his sisters; died of tuberculosis."[3] In 1848, the year after Emily published her great novel, Branwell took ill and died. Attending her brother's funeral on a cold, wet day, Emily fell ill and died of tuberculosis as well on December 19th of the same year. Emily Brontë was notoriously private, reserved, and stubborn; she refused any medical care until it was too late. So, the Brontë household knew much struggle, sickness, and death: Reverend Patrick outlived his wife and all his children.

---

3. Springfield, MA: G. & C. Merriam and Co., 1961, p. 197.

WHAT OTHER NOTABLES SAID

"*Wuthering Heights* was hewn in a wild workshop, with simple tools, out of homely materials…. [Like a chiseled granite block, it] took human shape; and there it stands colossal, dark and frowning, half statue, half rock: in the former sense, terrible and goblin-like; in the latter, almost beautiful, for its colouring is of mellow grey, and moorland moss clothes it; and heath, with its blooming bells and balmy fragrance, grows faithfully close to the giant's foot."
~Charlotte Brontë, Preface to the 1850 edition

"[*Wuthering Heights*] is a fiend of a book—an incredible monster." ~Dante Gabriel Rossetti[4]

"(How shall I sing her?) whose soul
Knew no fellow for might,

4. George Birkbeck Hill, ed., *Letters of Dante Gabriel Rossetti to William Allingham* (New York: Frederick A. Stokes, 1897), 58 (DG Rossetti, 1854).

Passion, vehemence, grief,
Daring, since Byron died,
That world-famed son of fire—she, who sank
Baffled, unknown, self-consumed;
Whose too bold dying song
Stirr'd, like a clarion-blast, my soul."
~Matthew Arnold[5]

"Emily Brontë's mind was at once dark and luminous.... Her qualities were each and all splendid, but too massive and masculine for her frail frame, worn and worried by consumption. *Wuthering Heights* is a noble work. Frequent passages haunt one like scenes from *Macbeth*." ~William Russell[6]

"[*Wuthering Heights* is] essentially and definitely a poem in the fullest and most positive sense of the term." ~Algernon Swinburne[7]

"Emily Brontë was a wild, original, and striking creature, but her one book is a kind of prose 'Kubla Khan'—a nightmare of the superheated imagination." ~Frederic Harrison[8]

---

5. *Haworth Churchyard*, April 1855.

6. W.C. Russell, *The Book of Authors* (London: Frederick Warne and Co., 1871),499.

7. *The Athenaeum*, June 16, 1883.

8. Frederic Harrison, "Charlotte Brontë's Place in Literature," *The Forum*, Vol. 19: March-August 1895 (New York: The Forum Publishing, 1895), 32.

"[Emily Brontë's] imagination was sometimes super-human—always inhuman. *Wuthering Heights* might have been written by an eagle. She is the strongest instance of these strong imaginations that made the other sex [men] a monster: for Heathcliffe fails as a man as catastrophically as he succeeds as a demon." ~G. K. Chesterton[9]

"[*Wuthering Heights*] exerts great power over its readers in its own violence, and in its presentation of striking psychological, sociological, and natural detail." ~J. Hillis Miller[10]

9. *The Victorian Age in Literature* (London: Williams and Norgate, 1913), 113.

10. *Fiction and Repetition: Seven English Novels* (Cambridge, MA: Harvard University Press, 1982), 42.

SETTING, CHARACTERS, AND PLOT SUMMARY

Setting:

The action takes place in the desolate, isolated Yorkshire moorlands of Northern England between 1740 and 1803 at two country estates (Wuthering Heights and Thrushcross Grange) roughly four miles from each other. Envision a region of damp, rocky, rolling hills attacked by winds, obscured by fogs, and covered by large patches of grass and heather: "a perfect misanthropist's Heaven."[11] Again, from the novel: "'Wuthering' being a significant provincial adjective, descriptive of the atmospheric tumult to which its station is exposed in stormy weather ... one may guess the power of the north wind, blowing over the edge, by the excess slanting of a few stunted [fir trees] ... and by a range of gaunt thorns all stretching their limbs

---

11. All citations are from the Canon Classics Edition (Moscow: Canon Press, 2019), 1.

one way, as if craving alms of the sun" (2). The soil supports very little life due to its high acid content, killing off most vegetation and rendering it largely barren; what trees may grow are often twisted and set at awkward angles by the violent winds. The setting perfectly supports the many dark, mysterious, deadly, and haunting aspects of this gothic novel.

Main Characters:
Narrators

• **Mr. Lockwood:** Tenant of Thrushcross Grange driven by curiosity to know the recent history of Wuthering Heights estate four miles from him.

• **Ellen Dean:** Called Nelly. She served as housekeeper at Wuthering Heights, then nursemaid at Thrushcross Grange for Catherine (once Catherine married Edgar Linton and moved to Thrushcross). Nelly continued on at Thrushcross after the untimely death of Catherine.

At Wuthering Heights

• **Mr. and Mrs. Earnshaw** own Wuthering Heights; they have one adopted and two biological children. Mr. Earnshaw favors his adopted child, Heathcliff, arousing early antipathy from his other children. Mrs. Earnshaw dies within two years of adopting Heathcliff and Mr. Earnshaw dies some years later.

• **Hindley Earnshaw** resents and despises his adopted brother, Heathcliff. When Mr. Earnshaw dies, Hindley takes over the management of the household and forces Heathcliff into menial labor. At college, Hindley meets and then marries Frances (who also mistreats Heathcliff). Frances dies after the birth of their son, **Hareton**.

• **Catherine (also called Miss Cathy) Earnshaw** is a secondary protagonist in the novel. At first she mistreats Heathcliff. Later, she warms, and finally falls in love with him; however, calculating by social and material advantage, she marries her neighbor Edgar Linton, driving Heathcliff nearly mad. Catherine and Edgar have one child, **Catherine Linton (also called Cathy)**.

• **Heathcliff** is the protagonist of the novel. Heathcliff's life began as an orphaned street child in Liverpool. He is adopted by Mr. Earnshaw. Life at Wuthering Heights is challenging for him, and he grows up simultaneously spoiled and proud (from Mr. Earnshaw), yet despised and rejected (especially by Hindley). He falls in love with Catherine but cannot marry her. Much of the novel revolves around Heathcliff's actions driven by vengeance on Hindley (for his abuse) and Catherine (for choosing Edgar as her husband). He marries Isabella Linton and they have one child, a boy, **Linton**.

• **Zillah:** Housekeeper at Wuthering Heights.

• **Joseph:** Contentious old servant at Wuthering Heights. He is harsh, ignorant, violent, and puritanical—Brontë's caricature of rude country religion.

At Thrushcross Grange

• **Mr. and Mrs. Linton** own Thrushcross Grange and have two children, Edgar and Isabella. They are generally a more orderly and decorous household than the Earnshaws but show little wisdom beyond their neighbors as both children make unfortunate marriage decisions.

• **Edgar** marries Catherine Earnshaw, incurring the wrath of Heathcliff.

• **Isabella** is later courted by Heathcliff. He marries her to spite Catherine and the Lintons; he treats Isabella wretchedly. Isabella finally flees Heathcliff's abuse.

• **Mr. Kenneth:** Doctor who attends the young, distressed, dying mother, Catherine.

Plot

The story opens as a diary entry from Mr. Lockwood dated 1801. Lockwood is the new tenant of Thrushcross Grange and decides to visit his landlord, Heathcliff Earnshaw, a few miles away at Wuthering Heights. The opening chapters show Lockwood to be educated and curious as well as hasty and bumbling; not an entirely reliable narrator. He readily imposes on others without invitation and quickly makes assumptions about them. But his mix of apparent social advantage (at least enough to lease Thrushcross Grange) and impudent curiosity provide the kind of character who could crack into the fiercely private household at Wuthering Heights and relay the story to the reader.

Lockwood's first visit to Wuthering Heights is awkward and tense; heedless of the negative signs, he returns days later uninvited, foolishly jumping the fence to demand an audience with his landlord again. Lockwood is generally ignored by the household (though the dogs attack him) but realizes that he must remain at Wuthering Heights that night due to bad weather. Zillah, the maid, puts Lockwood in Catherine's childhood room, admonishing Lockwood not to let his presence there be known to Heathcliff.

That night, Lockwood has a nightmare and is wakened by a tree branch and its cones rapping the window in the wind. The window is soldered shut, so, in his sleepy stupor, he smashes the pane in order to break the branch and silence the noise. But when he grabs the branch, he finds it actually a small, cold hand tightly clamping his: Catherine Earnshaw's ghost! She begs to be let in, claiming that she must return home. Lockwood says he needs his arm free to assist her, and when she releases it, he piles books in front of the window and tells her he'll never let her in. His yelling finally draws Heathcliff, who is infuriated that Lockwood should be there in Catherine's old room. But Heathcliff shifts from choking wrath to passionate dismay as he begs Catherine's spirit to join him in the house, all to no avail.

When Lockwood returns to Thrushcross Grange, he inquires of Ellen Dean (Nelly) concerning the history of Heathcliff and Wuthering Heights. Since Nelly had spent her years at Wuthering Heights and Thrushcross Grange, she makes an ideal source. Nelly recounts the previous forty-year history which Mr. Lockwood eventually writes out.

Thirty years ago, Heathcliff was a street urchin adopted by the owners of Wuthering Heights, Mr. and Mrs. Earnshaw. Mrs. Earnshaw dies soon after adopting the boy, and Mr. Earnshaw's doting over Heathcliff arouses fierce jealousy in Hindley Earnshaw, who routinely abuses his taciturn adoptive brother. Though Catherine immediately dislikes Heathcliff, that reverses over time into deep friendship, even romantic friendship as they spend many hours in each other's company; however, she refuses to consider marrying Heathcliff on account of his poor education and prospects, eventually preferring the material and social advantages promised by Edgar Linton, the heir of neighboring Thrushcross Grange.

Once Mr. Earnshaw dies, Hindley and his wife, Frances, lord their place over Heathcliff and continue to humiliate him, stirring vengeance in his heart. The table begins to turn on Hindley, however, as his young wife dies after giving birth to their son, Hareton. Hindley develops into a raging drunk. Heathcliff leaves the region heartbroken over Catherine's refusal to consider him in marriage, returning three years later with mysteriously acquired wealth, but finding Catherine now married to Edgar Linton. Heathcliff sets into motion a diabolical stratagem for revenge on those who dashed his young hopes. Heathcliff marries Edgar's sister, Isabella, simply to abuse her and spite the alliance of Edgar and Catherine. Simultaneously, Heathcliff secretly buys Wuthering Height's mortgage to secure his power over the Earnshaw heirs.

Catherine falls ill. Heathcliff visits his one-time love, and the two seem mad with regret, longing desperately for one another. Weakened Catherine then dies giving birth to a daughter. The child is named Catherine after her departed mother (rather confusing for the reader, though). Heathcliff steals into the house to visit Catherine's corpse before it is buried, opens the locket about her neck, and casts Edgar's lock of hair out, replacing it with his own dark hair. Ellen later mingles the rivals' locks of hair and seals them up in the locket. Isabella flees her hateful husband Heathcliff, though she is pregnant with his child. She gives birth to a son.

Twelve years later, Isabella dies, and Linton ends up with his father, Heathcliff. By now, Hindley Earnshaw has died, so Heathcliff is raising both his son, Linton, and his nephew, Hareton. He treats his nephew harshly, taking special pride in providing little social or academic education to him, ensuring a barbaric and uncouth end to the Earnshaw line. Heathcliff's final move will be to force (by kidnapping and abusing) young Cathy (we'll call her Cathy to distinguish her from the deceased Catherine) to marry his son Linton, thereby denying future fortunes to all other heirs (adopted brother Hindley's son Hareton in deep debt to him and brother-in-law Edgar's daughter married to his son, thereby transferring Thrush-cross Grange to his line). When his son, Linton, dies and leaves everything to Heathcliff (all part of the monster's wicked plan), he imagines victory: death of his enemies and ownership of both estates.

But instead of gleeful glory, Heathcliff is losing his mind, seeing visions of Catherine, hoping for his own death to meet her, and forgoing food. Cathy and Hareton develop a close friendship. She recognizes the good beneath the vulgar training of her cousin. One day, Heathcliff is found dead in his room, apparently due to the intense soul struggle. Heathcliff is buried next to Catherine and Edgar Earnshaw. His wicked stratagem, though causing great harm and death, finally fails: Cathy and Hareton are due to marry soon. The best and most gracious of the Earnshaw and Linton lines lives on in mutual love and delight with no fear of restless ghosts, vengeful tyrants, or estate issues.

WORLDVIEW ANALYSIS

Though earth and man were gone,
And suns and universes ceased to be,
And Thou were left alone,
Every existence would exist in Thee.

There is no room for Death,
Nor atom that his might could render void:
Thou—Thou art Being and Breath,
And what Thou art may never be destroyed.[12]

Shady Sympathies

The intellectual core of *Wuthering Heights* is readily understood through the character Heathcliff. Heathcliff is a

---

12. From Emily Brontë's last poem, see *The Sisters Bronte* (Toronto: Random House Canada, 2015), 170. As Brontë approaches death, the mighty powers she seemed to grant Catherine and Heathcliff's soul(s) are rendered instead to God.

monster, a bestial predator: "It's odd what a savage feeling I have to anything that seems afraid of me!" (272). He savors others' suffering: "Had I been born where laws are less strict, and tastes less dainty, I should treat myself to a slow vivisection of [Cathy and Linton] as an evening's amusement" (272). Yet Heathcliff also possesses a powerful bond of devotion to the woman he longs for, Catherine Earnshaw. When she dies, he exclaims, "Oh, God! it is unutterable! I *cannot* live without my life! I *cannot* live without my soul!" (169). How can the same character show such cruelty and such devotion; what is the reader to make of Heathcliff's character?

Brontë forged his nature under the auspices of her immediate literary predecessors hailing from what we now term the Romantic genre and its darker subgenre, Gothic. Thus, Heathcliff displays an uncertain pedigree, supernatural connections, violent eruptions, and thirst for vengeance, such as one finds in Mary Shelley's "creature" in *Frankenstein*. Heathcliff also features the brooding, tortured, cunning, immoral, and domineering anti-heroic qualities which make up a Byronic hero, such as Manfred,[13] forged in the furnace of a passionate moral tension. Thus, although *Wuthering Heights* features fewer supernatural elements and slightly less dramatic immorality than some of its Gothic predecessors and heirs, it does

---

13. The main character in Byron's 1817 work *Manfred: A Dramatic Poem*.

fit squarely in the tradition, stylistically.[14] Consequently, many of the issues that arise in *Wuthering Heights* are common to Gothic productions, chief of which is the spiritual vision the story relates.

In *Wuthering Heights*, the plotline is reasonable enough: two characters sin egregiously against themselves and others and die prematurely. The moral justice implied by the plotline probably kept its early critics from fighting too long against the depictions of infidelity, violence, and child abuse drawn throughout the text. The Bible, Sophocles, Shakespeare, Flannery O'Connor, and C.S. Lewis all present the reader with characters engaged in dark acts worse than Brontë depicts, yet there is still a fatal moral concern in Brontë's work: the progression of character and plot development seem to obscure rather than clarify moral meaning. This is evident in the sympathy most readers develop for Heathcliff,[15] a living demon who rules

14. The Gothic genre was established by Horace Walpole's *The Castle of Otranto* (1765) featuring an ancient castle, a threatened maiden, a driven villain, and a dark, supernatural curse brooding over the tale. In *Wuthering Heights*, the Gothic designation derives from the decaying estate, cursed families, villainous revenge, ghostly apparitions, and intense, even supernatural bond expressed by Catherine for Heathcliff, and vice versa.

15. The moral issue is easiest to recognize when one considers noble and ignoble characters in other classic tales. Iago's betrayal in *Othello*, for instance, is loathsome; he lurks about the mind like a vile, limping spider. Or, in *That Hideous Strength*, what does St. Anne's leader Elwin Ransom even do? Yet, it will not take the reader long to understand that Ransom's strange soul is infinitely more beautiful, valuable, and

over others violently, planning their deaths by suffocating depression and heartbreak, even abusing children, and openly yearning to cut their living bodies apart. Yet, rather than viewing this character reasonably, so many readers simply recall Heathcliff as the passionate romantic epitome of tall, dark, and handsome. How is this possible? First, Brontë shows the reader a young Heathcliff, orphaned and abused by his adopted brother. Second, the reader watches his young heart break when being denied in love. These details provide a plausible motivational background for him. Finally, Heathcliff's Nietzschean strength of will and determination to be with Catherine look like devoted love. Who can deny such absolute love?

This, then, is the mortal sin of a great deal of literature, especially Romantic and Gothic literature to this day: sympathy is often developed for evil ideas, characters, and their actions. And so we witness the public's regular penchant for the next book or movie installment of *Fifty Shades of the Next Most Shocking Sin We Privately Feel Like Entertaining.* The question in all of this is of the heart: where are our sympathies?

Heathcliff and Catherine do not know or experience true love because what they call love is rooted in selfishness and envy; their love is never patient or kind. It ignores biblical counsel and so fails miserably, however heartfelt the declarations appear. Great literature may

---

imitable than Frost or Filostrato, however progressive, powerful, successful, or intelligent they may seem.

include immoral situations and characters. It may depict darkly supernatural events and ambiguous characters, but, in the finest literature, the unfolding of character and plot elucidates moral reality. Thus, there are two paths to take when morally interpreting *Wuthering Heights*. An unprofitable path openly or secretly admires the relationship shared between Heathcliff and Catherine. A profitable path recognizes a falsehood and considers the collateral damage, however passionately displayed—then laughs.

Heretical Hearts

So, if Catherine and Heathcliff's passion is not founded in Christian union, how is it formed? Consider Catherine's thoughts to Nelly immediately after accepting Edgar Linton's proposal of marriage:

> My great thought in living is [Heathcliff]. If all else perished, and *he* remained, *I* should still continue to be; and if all else remained, and he were annihilated, the universe would turn to a mighty stranger: I should not seem a part of it.—My love for Linton is like the foliage in the woods: time will change it, I'm well aware, as winter changes the trees. My love for Heathcliff resembles the eternal rocks beneath: a source of little visible delight, but necessary. Nelly, I *am* Heathcliff! He's always, always in my mind: not as a pleasure, any more than I am always a pleasure to myself, but as my own being. (83)

Catherine is marrying Edgar Linton for the stability it should bring all the people at Wuthering Heights and Thrushcross Grange, but she is still obsessed with Heathcliff and imagines no culpable conflict in promising divided conjugal allegiances. The culture of the age (and every age?) was replete with examples of sideline liaisons, particularly among young ladies with little opportunity to produce a living income and pressured to use marriage to secure comfort and fortune for their families, so the dire confusion of this fifteen-year-old girl is understandable. The problem is that the progressing novel employs these scenes to exhibit the white heat of passion rather than to correct preceding confusion.

The idea that Love commands us and that we have little say in the matter is old and will remain with us as long as sin endures. Many people long for a perfect soul-mate to magically appear, banish their loneliness, and bring them true fulfillment in perfect romantic union. In short, they want salvation through romantic passion, which is a dead-end. And, more shrewdly, true love defined by our present feeling or state of mind is simply a convenient way to excuse unfaithfulness. Catherine and Heathcliff may be physically chaste, but they are emotionally adulterous, giving to one another what is rightly due to their lawful spouses.

Catherine's heart takes this a step further: what if their love were excusable, not simply because it is unalterable, but because it isn't finally temporal love, but a spiritual union of the soul, unrelated to any physical or temporal bounds? Heathcliff knows he is doing wrong in hateful revenge. Catherine seems to see no issue with her idolatrous view of Heathcliff because she doesn't view her relationship to Heathcliff simply as love, but as identity,[16] something she sees as transcending earthly love: "[Heathcliff's] more myself than I am. Whatever our souls are made of, his and mine are the same" (81). Catherine thinks she has the advantage of union with Heathcliff regardless of any formal relationship, so she is free to marry in whatever way will bring the most advantage. Heathcliff, on the other hand, won't be led so readily philosophically misled. Catherine seems to believe their love can endure by positing a gnostic division between the true/spiritual/emotional/soulmate/Heathcliff and the false/physical/temporal/husband/Edgar, but this a just an old Gnostic heresy redressed in her own circumstances.[17] Heathcliff balks at her suggestion; he wants a total union[18] and views her marriage to Edgar as a hideous lie to both men. He

16. Interestingly, there is a parallel with the gay agenda today. The modern conversation is steered away from moral truth (which the Bible answers clearly) to personal identity (if a person is made gay, how can one deny it?). Thus, some looked for a genetic difference in homosexuals; that failing, most fall back on the fallacy that people have the absolute right to define themselves. But we are made in God's image, so He has the ultimate right to define us, despite our proclivities or perversities.

17. Gnosticisim was a third-century Christian heresy that maintained that the body and all the material world were evil, and that salvation consisted of one's soul escaping from the body.

18. For instance, when Catherine dies, Heathcliff must see the body, and when Heathcliff makes arrangements for his own burial, he demands to be buried by Catherine, that they might mingle in their decay.

is not initially satisfied by Catherine's spiritual vision of their union.

In chapter XV, Catherine lies on her deathbed, and a distraught Heathcliff denies her romantic vision, desperate that she should fight to stay with the living. But Catherine's confidence in her own vision seems boundless: "That is not *my* Heathcliff. I shall love mine yet; and take him with me: he's in my soul" (162). She will deny the very form before her, believing in the truer Heathcliff she takes with her into the afterlife. Thus, Brontë gives Catherine's fateful words, "I *am* Heathcliff," (83) a demonic resonance in the text. Catherine tells Heathcliff: "'I wish I could hold you,' she continued, bitterly, 'till we were both dead! I shouldn't care what you suffered. I care nothing for your sufferings. Why shouldn't you suffer? I do!'" (160). Heathcliff responds (with uncharacteristic reason): "'Are you possessed with a devil?'" Catherine breaks down, moaning, begging forgiveness (161). Heathcliff denies her plea for forgiveness: "I forgive what you have done to me. I love *my* murderer—but *yours*! How can I?" (163). He sees that Catherine's marital lie has slain her, and he can't forgive her for it. Catherine and Heathcliff's vision of love is clouded by anger, driven by envy, fueled by bitterness, and rooted more in selfish possession rather than humble sacrifice. Heathcliff must leave, and Catherine soon dies, but the melodramatic zenith is still to come.

When word reaches Heathcliff of Catherine's death, Heathcliff embraces significant tenants of Catherine's heretical vision, yet he acts them out through the hateful heat of his own temperament:

> 'May she wake in torment!' he cried, with frightful vehemence, stamping his foot, and groaning in a sudden paroxysm of ungovernable passion.... 'And I pray one prayer—I repeat it till my tongue stiffens—Catherine Earnshaw, may you not rest as long as I am living; you said I killed you—haunt me, then! The murdered *do* haunt their murderers, I believe. I know that ghosts *have* wandered on earth. Be with me always—take any form—drive me mad.... I *cannot* live without my soul!' (169)

Notice, particularly, the conclusion; he agrees that their souls are one, but rather than forgiveness (which she asked for), he hopes to harness the powers of a curse to reunite them. He won't accept Christian faith, but he does claim elsewhere to "have a strong faith in ghosts" and has a "conviction that they can, and do, exist among us!" (291). Thus, Heathcliff and Catherine's spiritual belief acknowledges an afterlife for the soul but is not Christian. Their vision is self-made, perhaps borrowing from the Spiritualistic philosophy popular with Victorian elites that emphasized direct communication with the spirit world to attain needful knowledge of life or God. Parallel to such a heresy, Heathcliff scoffs at eternal damnation and seeks a means of openly communicating with Catherine and "dissolving with her" (291). This reinforces the false assumptions on the nature of the soul that fifteen-year-old Catherine announced. Heathcliff shows himself a devoted catechumen to her false faith. The end thereof? Death, of course.

Taken as a whole, *Wuthering Heights* is an alchemical work, distilling the passionate attachment of young love into a dark, bitter cocktail. Why so bitter? Only Brontë knows her full reason, but it is little wonder that her creation remains with us, for people have long pondered dark romances cutting life short—especially the romance of youth—when it seems passion's blaze can burn without age's typical tempering effects (such as experience, self-awareness, and caution). Romeo and Juliet needed nothing but a few moments of consideration to gain their happiness; happiness that a few moments of that heated passion never truly achieves. And long after the world forgets the troubled lineage of King Arthur or which knight was worthy of the Holy Grail, men and women still will remember that fairy fantasy ended in a passionate storm surrounding Guinevere and Lancelot.

In this light, Brontë is perfectly justified in drawing her plot and characters as she did; what else could she do? Like race fans drawn to crashes, like moths drawn to flame, we are all drawn to and arrested by spectacle, whatever guise it visits us in. Young, passionate love is chief among such spectacles, as its human implications are so deep and generational, and its impulse beats within each of us.

Wuthering Heights can be an excellent text for high school students to read and recognize and give voice to passions their own hearts have hinted at, so long as it also serves as a testing and trying ground to forge a finer romantic vision than that known by the Earnshaws and Lintons. The key issue is romantic vision. Get that wrong, and the devils laugh as young lovers chase false fires through emotional swamps, no lover ever comparable to Heathcliff or Catherine's diabolic rapture. Get it right, the devils flee, and the firstfruits of passion are carefully cultivated to produce a wine of wisdom. A right vision recognizes the necessity of real patience (rather than mere intuition) to form opinions and conclusions about value and character in relationships. A right vision can laugh a confident, joyful laugh at the challenges love brings (rather than a rebellious, arrogant, or cynical cackle) because a right vision knows and believes in God's grace as a stronger power than any other at work. A right romance jokes together over weeding and dishes (can we imagine Catherine and Heathcliff ever doing so?), knows and enjoys the daily ebbs and flows of life and love. Unadulterated romantic passion always leads to something adulterous because a virtuous love is found in good company (with the likes of humility and honor and cheer), and romantic love no less. Let that lesson remain with us, and *Wuthering Heights* will prove a blessing. Forget it, and we toil under Heathcliff's curse.

QUOTABLES

1. "For shame, Heathcliff!" said [Nelly]. "It is for God to punish wicked people; we should learn to forgive." ~Chapter VII, p. 61

2. "No, God won't have the satisfaction that I shall," he returned. "I only wish I knew the best way! Let me alone, and I'll plan it out: while I'm thinking of that I don't feel pain." ~Heathcliff, Chapter VII, p. 61

3. "It would degrade me to marry Heathcliff now; so he shall never know how I love him: and that, not because he's handsome, Nelly, but because he's more myself than I am. Whatever our souls are made of, his and mine are the same." ~Catherine, Chapter IX, p. 81

4. "My love for Heathcliff resembles the eternal rocks beneath: a source of little visible delight, but necessary. Nelly, I *am* Heathcliff!" ~Catherine, Chapter IX, p. 83

5. "Two words would comprehend my future–death and hell: existence, after losing her, would be hell. Yet I was a fool to fancy for a moment that she valued Edgar Linton's attachment more than mine. If he loved with all the powers of his puny being, he couldn't love as much in eighty years as I could in a day." ~Heathcliff, Chapter XIV, p. 150

6. "'Why did you despise me? Why did you betray your own heart, Cathy? I have not one word of comfort. You deserve this. You have killed yourself. Yes, you may kiss me, and cry; and wring out my kisses and tears: they'll blight you— they'll damn you. You loved me—then what right had you to leave me? What right—answer me—for the poor fancy you felt for Linton? Because misery and degradation, and death, and nothing that God or Satan could inflict would have parted us, you, of your own will, did it. I have not broken your heart—you have broken it; and in breaking it, you have broken mine.'" ~Heathcliff, Chapter XV, p. 163

7. "Let me alone. Let me alone," sobbed Catherine. "If I've done wrong, I'm dying for it. It is enough! You left me too: but I won't upbraid you! I forgive you. Forgive me!" ~Chapter XV, p. 163

8. "Kiss me again; and don't let me see your eyes! I forgive what you have done to me. I love *my* murderer—but *yours*! How can I?" ~Heathcliff, Chapter XV, p. 163

9. "The entire world is a dreadful collection of memoranda that she did exist, and that I have lost her!" ~Heathcliff, Chapter XXX, p. 328

21 SIGNIFICANT
QUESTIONS AND ANSWERS

1. Identify and explain a significant worldview issue in *Wuthering Heights*.

   Two significant issues are 1) Catherine and Heathcliff's heretical view of the nature of the soul and afterlife, 2) a misleading representation of passionate romance.

2. Explain the narrative framework of *Wuthering Heights*.

   Wuthering Heights is a frame narrative. The main tale is told by the housekeeper Nelly (Ellen Dean) through a written account by Mr. Lockwood. At times, Nelly is quoting other characters at length, or Lockwood is quoting from direct conversation with a character beside Nelly (such as Heathcliff). Also, the narration sometimes skips forward or backward. Thus, the narrative is challenging to follow at times.

3. How does the frame narrative affect the interpretation of *Wuthering Heights*?

> Frame narrating generally adds complexity and ambiguity to the work. In the case of this novel, we have a rather simple yet prudent first-hand account of many events (Nelly), told through the hand of a somewhat odd and peevish renter (Mr. Lockwood). Even though Nelly is a fairly sound depository for the tale, she only has limited access to the most private aspects of many characters (such as Heathcliff). The shifting times also requires the reader to keep various ages and stages of life in mind for the characters as the narrative shifts from present to past and back to present again.

4. Who are the protagonists and antagonists in the novel?

> Catherine and Heathcliff are both protagonists in the novel and serve as antagonists to themselves and one another. Catherine serves as antagonist to her and Heathcliff's happiness by marrying Edgar. Heathcliff serves as antagonist to Catherine by living out his revenge on her and her family while she lives. Once Catherine dies, her ghost seems to torment Heathcliff until the resolution when they apparently reunite in death. This scheme is debatable. One could make a case that Hindley and Catherine serve as antagonists to Heathcliff as protagonist.

5.   What does Heathcliff's name imply?

> Heathcliff's name implies a wild danger, an acidic
> soil where life cannot thrive, a wasteland of a life
> with a precipitous end.

6.   Why is *Wuthering Heights* considered a Gothic novel?

> *Wuthering Heights* is a Gothic novel because it shows
> so many elements typical of that genre, chiefly a ru-
> inous central estate, supernatural horrors, villainous
> schemes, mysterious family curses, and isolated char-
> acters and locales.

7.   Why is Wuthering Heights a fitting descriptor for the
     estate?

> The family is blasted by violent gales of emotion-
> al distress that twist and disfigure its members like
> gnarled trees exposed on a weather-beaten hill.

8.   Is Gothic fiction inherently wrong, evil, or misleading?

> No, Gothic fiction features a darker style but is not
> necessarily evil or misleading. It must be considered
> author by author and work by work.

9.   What is the difference between Gothic and horror
     literature?

> In some cases there is little difference. Generally,
> the difference is in the focus, duration, descriptions,
> and intensity of the characters' suffering. Gothic lit-

erature tends to deliver a kind of exciting disquiet through dark elements but may have any number of actual literary aims. Horror usually aims at absolute terror in a victim, often exhibiting a perverse delight in others' suffering. There is no place for the latter in a Christian's life. Horrific deeds and places may be entertained to help the heart understand the world aright, such as the shocking images of Hell given in the Bible. The distinction is in the aim and sympathies the literature delivers to the reader, and the aim and sympathy should never naturally gravitate toward exulting in a person's undoing.

10. Is it wrong for Christians to read Gothic or horror literature?

No, the generic labels cover too many types and qualities of literary production to judge them as one, but it is probably wrong to entertain them more often than many Christians realize. The underlying reason is that the basic premise behind a great deal of horror is that there is a spiritual world all around us, but there is no good God that cares for us or will help us. Horror essentially posits a universe controlled by Satan. Therefore, the character in a horror story has nowhere to turn, and the reader watches another soul tormented into destruction by sinister and uncontrollable forces. Obviously, those assumptions are lies and not a wise place for the Christian to dwell. Secondly, having posited a perverse spiritual order, horror usually continues on to revel in a perverse physical order, so it's not surprising that sexually perverse imagery features commonly in horror. Again, not something Christians should entertain. That said, meditating on a world or soul devoid of or declining God's care may cause our hearts to rush to Him all the more. Flannery O'Connor, Graham Greene, and others have successfully employed elements of horror and a dark, gothic nature to relate compelling narratives that encourage and instill moral truth. Therefore, drawing the line between the helpful and hurtful in Gothic literature requires sense and has some room for debate among believers. Also, some works, like *Wuthering Heights*, describe none of their horrors explicitly, so the Christian reader has much more license to enjoy the work and consider where it does or does not elucidate beauty, truth, and goodness.

11. So, is it wrong for Christians to read accounts of horrific pain or soul torment?

> No, if that were the case, we couldn't read the gospels. The emphasis must be placed on the sympathies the writer is working to communicate to the reader. Since this can't always be easily ascertained, we must be thoughtful in the selection of our reading material, especially when it involves violence and suffering.

12. If some works should be avoided for immorality encouraged in the reader, and *Wuthering Heights* encourages some false moral sympathies, should Christians avoid *Wuthering Heights*?

> No, Christians should not feel compunction about reading *Wuthering Heights*. This is true for two major reasons. 1) The horrific elements (such as child abuse) are not written in any way to excite or encourage the reader to enjoy or imitate them. In general, perversity is viewed as just that and not dwelt on at length. 2) In the case of the false sympathies for Heathcliff and for the love Heathcliff and Catherine believe they have created, it falls within the pale of misleading ideas Christians should be able identify, understand, and answer, of the variety Christians deal with on a daily basis in media and the arts.

13. What is the inciting incident (the narrative moment that sets off the rise to the climax) of the novel?

> The plot's inciting incident occurs when Catherine decides to marry Edgar, despite the fact that she has given her heart to Heathcliff. It's understandable, given the fact that she was then living under her brother, Hindley, who abused and threatened every evil on a daily basis. Thus, rationalizing the marriage, she tells Nelly that the match is okay as long as one thinks of it having "only to do with the present." Nelly responds, "Perfectly right! if people be right to marry only for the present" (80). Which, of course, they are not, as marriage is a solemn prom-

ise concerning one's future. The exact moment of the inciting incident is when she declares that she cannot marry Heathcliff (and Heathcliff, overhearing it, rushes off to devise revenge).

14. What is the climax?

The climax occurs when Catherine dies. At this point, it seems clear that Heathcliff will eventually "dissolve," and his nefarious plans with him.

15. What does Heathcliff hope will happen after Catherine's death?

He hopes to destroy the Earnshaw and Linton families (including his own son), manipulating them in such a manner that he would live alone owning both estates. To do this, he needs his niece Cathy to marry his sickly son, Linton. Linton would inherit her estate (Thrushcross Grange), and then Heathcliff could inherit it from his son after manipulating his son to will the estate to him (Heathcliff). This occurs, and Linton dies, leaving Heathcliff briefly over both estates. The victory is pyrrhic as Heathcliff dies soon after.

16. At the end, it appears that Heathcliff is not eating. Why is Nelly so concerned about this?

She worries that when Heathcliff dies, if it is ruled suicide by virtue of refusing food, he will not be allowed to be buried near the church.

17. What is Heathcliff's response to this?

> Heathcliff doesn't seem to care and tells her that she would simply need to dig up his body to place it next to Catherine. If Nelly refused, he would haunt her. Heathcliff demands that he be buried next to Catherine with his coffin side open so that his remains will mingle with hers.

18. What are some moral truths that *Wuthering Heights* communicates?

> One of the most important truths that *Wuthering Heights* communicates is that abuse is cyclical; one generation may carry and then inflict the type of suffering it once endured. This is clearly the case with Heathcliff.

> Another truth we find is that drunkenness hurts children, destroys fortunes, and curses households.

> Finally, a beautiful truth unfolds at the conclusion of the novel. When the revenge plot finally unravels and Hareton and Cathy unite, the reader understands that any generation can break the cycle of a family curse through forgiveness, kindness, generosity, and humble self-sacrifice.

19. What evidence does the text supply that Catherine and Heathcliff's souls will not be at peace?

> Nelly asks Mr. Lockwood, "Do you believe such people are happy in the other world, sir? I'd give a great deal to know." He declines answering her in person, but he adds his personal thought to the text, "Retracing the course of Catherine Linton, I fear we have no right to think she is; but we'll leave her with her Maker" (167). It's also true that the ghosts of Catherine and Heathcliff deeply frighten a young boy.

20. What evidence does the text supply that Catherine and Heathcliff's souls are indeed at rest?

> Overall, Brontë clearly hints at divine indulgence by offering many closing olive branches to the couple. First, Heathcliff's wicked designs fall dead with the passing of his son. Heathcliff himself will soon pass away, leaving the estate to the more promising union of young Hareton and Cathy (daughter of the deceased Catherine and Edgar Linton). Second, a frightened shepherd boy apparently witnesses the spirits of the couple abiding together under a tree: "There's Heathcliff and a woman yonder... 'un' I darnut pass 'em" (341). Given the context of the novel, one imagines the "woman" as Catherine (and not Heathcliff's wife, Isabella). Nelly, the maid of seemingly simple but often profound advice gives a parting word: "I believe the dead are at peace" (341). Finally, there is the grace of Brontë's closing line,

Lockwood's gravesite meditation over the three headstones of the Edgar, Catherine, and Heathcliff.

21. What do the final words of the novel imply (when Lockwood is visiting graves Heathcliff, Catherine, and Edgar)?

The final pages imply that all may be well with the world. The revenge plot has been foiled, the ghosts of the deceased appear to be at peace, and the curse will no longer hang over Hareton and Cathy's future: "I lingered round them, under that benign sky: watched the moths fluttering among the heath and harebells, listened to the soft wind breathing through the grass, and wondered how any one could ever imagine unquiet slumbers for the sleepers in that quiet earth" (342). It's not simply the imagery but all the whispering alliteration and assonance that supplies a concluding benediction of sweet rest to the work, amply and artfully demonstrating Brontë's poetic grace.

FURTHER DISCUSSION AND REVIEW

Master what you have read by reviewing and integrating the different elements of this classic.

SETTING AND CHARACTERS

How does the setting affect the development of plot and character in the novel? Be able to compare and contrast the personalities of the main characters and at least four minor characters. Do any characters change over the course of the novel? How? Are any characters heroic or admirable? Are any characters devoid of virtue? Are any characters humorous?

PLOT

Be able to describe the beginning, middle, and end of the book along with specific details that move the plot forward and make it compelling.

CONFLICT

Although we find violence, lies, abuse, manipulation, and death in this novel, a good case could be made that external conflict is eclipsed by internal conflict. Explain.

THEME STATEMENTS

Be able to describe what this classic is telling us about the world. Is the message true? What truth can we take from the plot, characters, conflict, and themes (even if the author didn't believe that truth)? Do any objects take on added meaning because of repetition or their place in the story (i.e., do any objects become symbols)? How does the author use perspective, tone, and irony to tell the truth?

> Often in literature, nature and character are mirrored. Consider how the moors and estates reflect various characters, especially main characters.

> Sin's consequences go beyond ourselves and affect others, especially our children (Num. 14:18). How does this theme show itself in the novel? What is the way out of the sad cycle? Is the cycle broken in the novel?

> "For love is as strong as death,/ Jealousy as cruel as the grave;/ Its flames are flames of fire,/ A most vehement flame" (Song of Solomon 8:6). How might love be stronger than death and jealously cruel as the grave in this work? Consider Catherine

and Heathcliff, of course. Can you discover other examples?

What is love? *Wuthering Heights* encourages the reader to consider the right uses and potential abuses of love, especially romantic love. What can the reader learn about true love by considering the novel in light of God's Word?

"'Vengeance is Mine, I will repay,' says the Lord" (Rom. 12:19). Vengeance is a significant theme in *Wuthering Heights*. When does it begin, how does it operate, and what are its effects?

Dark, even demonic, forces appear to be at work throughout the novel. Provide examples and consider what dispels those evil forces.

A NOTE FROM THE PUBLISHER:
TAKING THE CLASSICS QUIZ

Once you have finished the worldview guide, you can prepare for the end-of-book test. Each test will consist of a short-answer section on the book itself and the author, a short-answer section on plot and the narrative, and a long-answer essay section on worldview, conflict, and themes.

Each quiz, along with other helps, can be downloaded for free at www.canonpress.com/ClassicsQuizzes. If you have any questions about the quiz or its answers or the Worldview Guides in general, you can contact Canon Press at service@canonpress.com or 208.892.8074.

ABOUT THE AUTHOR

Marcus Schwager holds a Master's degree in Humanities from California State University, Dominguez Hills, writing his thesis on G. K. Chesterton. He and his wife, Meris, have five children and attend Trinity Covenant Church in Aptos, California. He writes for Canon Press, teaches upper-school Humanities at St. Abraham's Classical Christian Academy, and works for his family's construction and real estate company.

www.ingramcontent.com/pod-product-compliance
Lightning Source LLC
Chambersburg PA
CBHW071933020426
42331CB00010B/2857